Fly a Plane

with Captain Jack

Author: John Pullen

ISBN-13: 978-1984908629

ISBN-10: 1984908626

Copyright © 2018 John Pullen

Publisher: John Pullen

All rights reserved. No part of this publication may be reproduced, stored in a retrieval system or transmitted in any form or by any means, electronic, mechanical, photocopying, recording or otherwise, without the prior written permission of the copyright owner of this book.

First Print Edition: 2018

Printed by Createspace an Amazon company

Cover Image Design: Jag_cz

Captain Jack Image: Inllusion

www.johnpullenwriter.com

For

Emma

Contents

Flight Plan	11
Pre-Flight Checks	16
The Cockpit	22
Jet Engines	32
Engine Start	36
Taxi	40
Take-Off and Climb	45
Climbing to Cruising Altitude	50
On-Route Cruising	54
Pressurisation and Air Conditioning	57
Fuel Management	62
Electrical System	66
Fire Protection Systems	69
Navigation	73
Communications	78
Descent	82
Landing	90

Arrival and Deplaning	99
Further Knowledge	104
Principles of Flight	107
Answers to the Questions	115

Captain Jack says…

"The Best Office in the World"

Flight Plan

It is very early in the morning but for Captain Jack, his new working day has already started. For today Captain Jack is going to fly his airliner from London to Athens in Greece. Captain Jack is an airline pilot and he will be in charge of flying 200 passengers to their destination.

He quickly has a shower and then puts on his airline pilot's uniform. It has black trousers and a black jacket. On his sleeves he has four gold stripes. This tells everybody that Jack is a Captain. He also wears four gold stripes or bars on the shoulders of his white shirt and just above his left hand breast pocket he wears the gold wings of a pilot. He is very proud of these. Finally he puts on his hat which also has gold wings just above the peak.

Captain Jack gets into his car and drives to the airport. It does not take him very long as he must make sure that he always lives less than an hour away. This is so he can get to the airport quickly if another pilot is ill and cannot fly his plane. Jack is able to park his car in a special car park reserved for pilots and other people who work for the airline.

The first place Jack has to go is called the Crew Briefing Room. It is in here that he will be able to look at his Flight Plan. This is a document which tells Jack everything he needs to know about his flight. But Jack has already seen a copy. He has a computer tablet and he has logged on to the airline website so he can see a copy of his plan.

Pilots Preparing a Flight Plan
The Captain (left) has Four Gold Bars
The First Officer has Three Gold Bars

In the Crew Briefing Room he is joined by his friend and fellow pilot Alisha. She will be his co-pilot or First Officer on this flight. Because she is also very experienced, she has three gold stripes on the sleeves of her uniform. If for any reason Captain Jack was ill on the flight, First Officer Alisha would be able to fly and land the aeroplane safely on her own. Although Jack and Alisha have flown together many times, it is not unusual for two pilots to meet for the first time just before flying together. This is not a problem as each has been trained exactly the same way and so they will always work as a good team.

Jack and Alisha study the Flight Plan together. First they check the route they are going to fly. Then they check to see if the weather is going to be fine for the whole of the journey. Most of the time their aircraft will be flying above the clouds but they have to check if there are any strong winds which might affect them. They also check to see if the weather will be good when they land.

One of Captain Jack's most important jobs is to work out how much fuel he needs for the flight. He cannot tell the fuel tanker person to "Fill it up" because that might make the plane too heavy and be wasteful. So he carefully calculates how much he will need.

First Jack works out how much he will need taxiing out to the runway. Then he has to decide on how much he will need for the journey itself which includes the plane climbing and descending. The climbing and descending part is known as Burn-Off Fuel. Finally he has to make sure he has enough fuel in case of any problems. This might include diverting to another airport or having to circle above an airport if there is a queue of planes in front of him. Although there are other papers he must check, soon everything looks good and Captain Jack is able to accept the Flight Plan.

Captain Jack's Questions

"Which room do pilots meet in and check their Flight Plan?"

"How many gold stripes does a Captain have?"

"What things do pilots check on their Flight Plan?"

"What does Burn-Off Fuel mean?"

Pre-Flight Checks

As soon as the flight plan has been approved, Captain Jack and Alisha are ready to go out to their aeroplane. A small minibus is waiting for them but first they must go through security checks just like the passengers. However there is a special area for aircrews, so there is not much queuing. Both Jack and Alisha have special Identity Cards with their photograph attached. This proves to the security people that they are both pilots working for their airline.

They climb aboard their minibus outside the security building and soon they are crossing the apron to where their plane is waiting. Soon they see the brightly coloured tail of the aircraft and on the sides of the fuselage are painted their airline name – Fast World Airlines.

There is a lot of activity going on around the plane. The fuel tanker has arrived and the refueller is already fitting the fuel hoses to the underside of one of the wings. A modern airliner has a number of different fuel tanks but they are mostly located inside the wings.

If you ever watch a car being refuelled you will see that the pump can deliver a litre of fuel every few seconds. But the tanker is much quicker and an airliner needs a lot of fuel. In fact the tanker can deliver up to 3,000 litres a minute into the tanks.

Fuel is Pumped into Tanks in the Wings

Jack and Alisha go on board and find that the cabin crew have already arrived. The job of the cabin crew is not just to look after the passengers by supplying them with food and drinks during the flight. They also have to check that the aircraft is clean and tidy and that nothing has been left behind which could be suspicious.

Cargo, Luggage and Food are Loaded Aboard

They are also in charge of opening and closing the doors before and after a flight. But their most important job is to help passengers to safety in the very unlikely chance of there being a problem with the aircraft. All cabin crew are highly trained and know what to do in any emergency affecting the cabin and passengers. This allows the pilots to concentrate on flying the aircraft.

The person in charge of the cabin crew is called the Cabin Services Manager or CSM and today it is Suki who is in charge. She has been a manager for a few years and both Jack and Alisha know her and have flown with her many times.

There are three other cabin crew on the flight today. They are Mohammed, Amy and Michael. Mohammed and Amy are experienced air stewards but this is Michael's first trip as a trained cabin crew member. He is a little bit nervous but the others will help him if he needs it.

Captain Jack says he will brief Suki about their flight. Then she will brief the rest of the cabin crew so everybody will know what to expect. Because Captain Jack will be busy with Suki, Alisha will check the outside of the aircraft.

Inspecting the plane from the outside is a very important part of each flight. Although Alisha knows that some of the ground engineers will have checked the aircraft, it is still the duty of one of the pilots to make a final check before take-off.

This inspection is also called a Walk-Round and some of the things Alisha will be checking for are if any of the aircraft panels have been damaged. It is always possible that a passing vehicle may have bumped into the plane. This is very unlikely but Alisha wants to make sure.

She also checks that all the covers have been removed from the outside sensors. If they were to be left on then some of the instruments such as the airspeed indicators will not work correctly. She checks the tyres to make sure they are fully inflated and also that the undercarriage locking pins have been removed. When she is happy that everything is in order, she re-joins Jack in the cockpit.

Captain Jack's Questions

"Which airline do Captain Jack and Alisha work for?"

"Where in the aircraft are the main fuel tanks located?"

"How fast can fuel be pumped into the fuel tanks?"

"What is Suki's job title?"

"How many cabin crew are on board?"

"What is the outside inspection of the aircraft called?"

The Cockpit

Being the captain, Jack sits in the left-hand seat and Alisha, as the first officer, in the right-hand one. In front of them, above them and in between their seats are lots of screens, switches and levers. This is the cockpit of a modern jet airliner. At first, it all looks very complicated but is in fact a lot simpler than you might think.

Many older airliners were more complicated because they had many more separate instruments to check. But the modern cockpit uses video screens just like your computer or tablet. The screens are able to show lots of information which means less separate instruments are needed. Both Jack and Alisha have two identical screens side by side in front of them.

The one on the left is called the Primary Flight Display or PFD. This tells the pilots what attitude the aircraft is flying in. In the middle of the screen are a couple of lines which represent the aircraft. They are positioned against another line which shows the horizon. If the horizon bar moves down, it means the aircraft is climbing and if the horizon bar moves up, it means the plane is descending. If the horizon bar rotates it tells the pilots that the aircraft is turning. And Jack and Alisha will know all this without having to look out of the window.

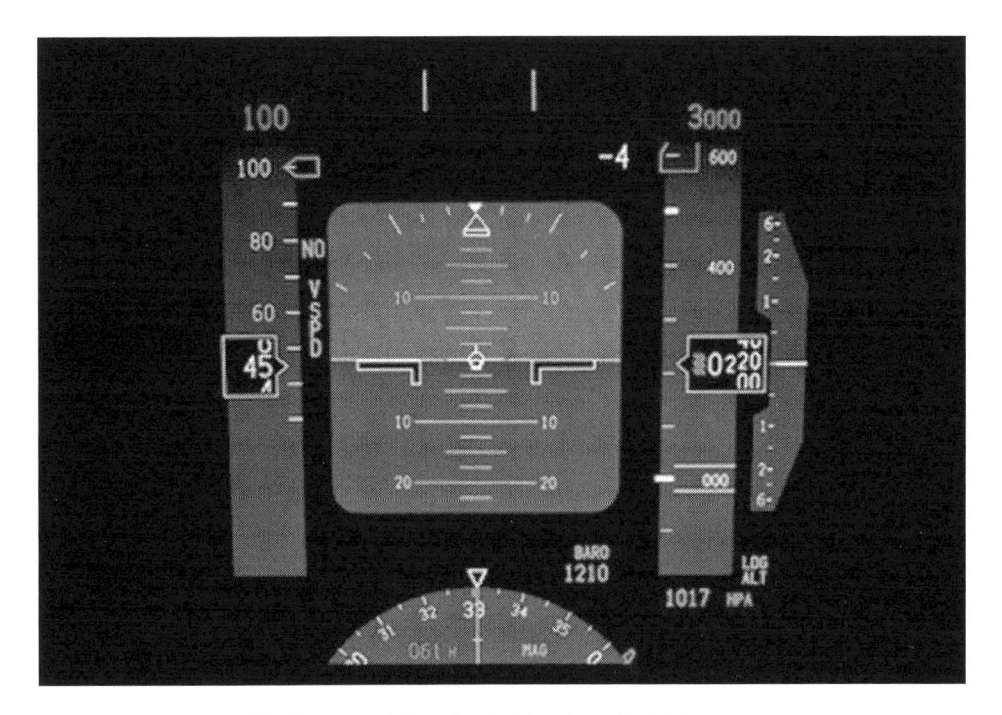

Primary Flight Display PFD

To the sides of each screen are numbers which tell Jack and Alisha how fast they are going and how high they are. And if they need it, they can get more information about how the airliner is flying from the same screen. For example at the top of the screen the state of the autopilot

23

can be checked. There is also a radio compass at the bottom of the screen.

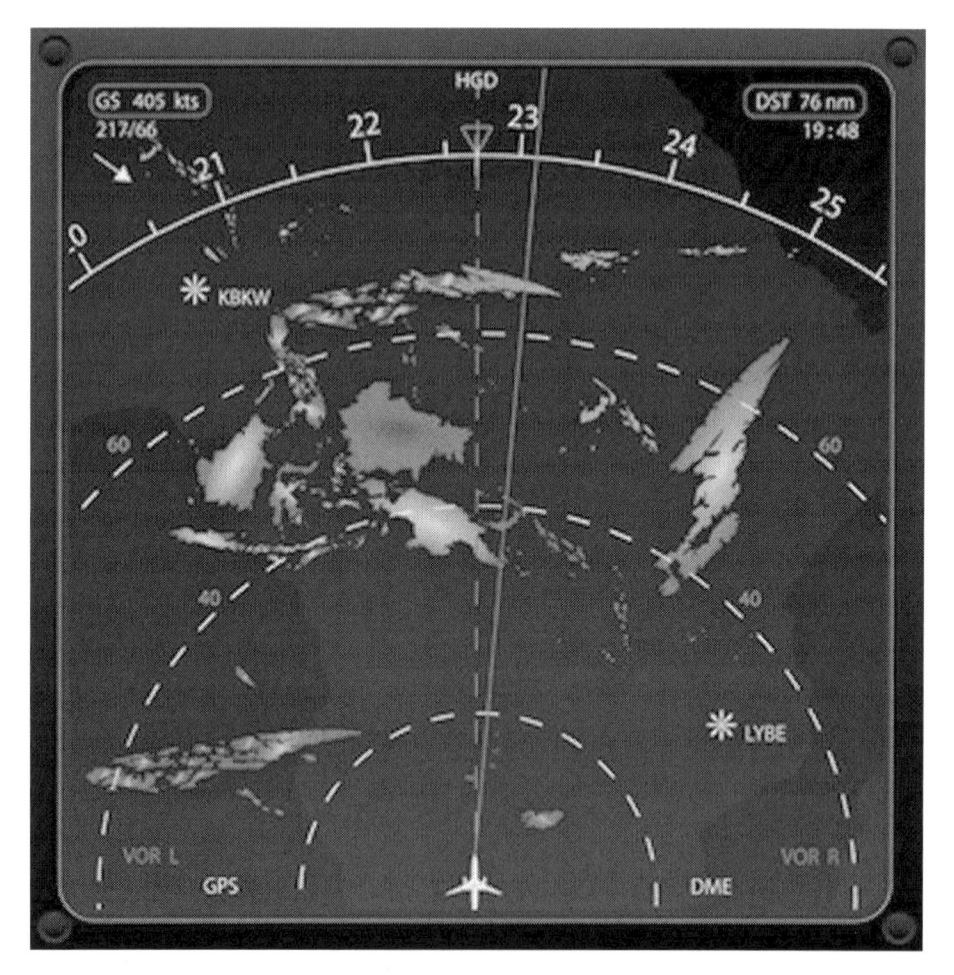

Navigation Display ND

On the right of the Primary Flight Display is the Navigation Display or ND. This tells the pilots about the

route they are flying from their departure airport to their destination. In this case it will be from London to Athens.

A symbol of the aircraft is shown in the bottom centre of the screen. Above it are a couple of curved lines. These represent distances the plane has to fly.

At the top of the screen is another curved line. It has numbers on it and it rotates when the plane turns. It is a modern version of a compass and tells Jack and Alisha in which direction they are flying. And like other compasses it uses the Magnetic North Pole rather than the Geographic North Pole to give directions.

However, this screen tells them a lot more than just direction and distance flown. It can also show what the weather is like up ahead. Clouds of different colours can be displayed in front of the aircraft symbol. The colours are green, yellow and red.

If Captain Jack sees red clouds on his screen, it means there is very bad weather ahead of them and he will probably change course in order to avoid them. On some of the latest navigation displays, the pilots are also told how high the clouds are so they may change altitude to avoid them. It means the passengers should enjoy a nice smooth flight.

Engine/Warning Display EWD (Centre)
Undercarriage Lever (Right of EWD)
Systems Display SD (Below EWD)
Multi-Functional Displays MFD (Left & Right of SD)

In the centre of the instrument panel is a single display called the Engine/Warning Display or EWD. It is split into two halves. The upper part of the screen tells Jack and Alisha everything they need to know about how each engine is working. If a problem should arise, then the lower half of the screen will tell them both what the problem is and then they can set about fixing it.

Below the EWD there is another screen. This is the Systems Display or SD and it can show the pilots how all the aircraft's systems are operating. These can include the amount and flow of fuel, the pressurisation of the aircraft and even the tyre pressures amongst many other systems.

Both Jack and Alisha have their own computer terminals to the side of them located on the centre console. They look a bit like a computer tablet with a small screen and a keyboard below. Each is called a Multi-Functional Display or MFD and it allows Jack and Alisha to monitor and make changes to aspects of the flight if they wish to.

There are a number of other controls and we shall see what they do later on in the flight. But before that, there is one other very important control we will look at. It is the Control Column. It used to be called a "Joystick" by pilots many years ago and it is the means by which Jack and Alisha can control the aircraft's movements. On older aircraft, the control column was fitted centrally in front of each pilot. But today, it is often to be found to the side of each pilot and it looks just like the old joystick on a home computer.

When the aircraft is in flight, if the stick is pulled back, the plane will climb higher whilst pushing it forward causes the aircraft to descend lower. If it is moved to the left, the aircraft will begin to roll and turn to the left and if pushed to the right, the plane will roll and turn to the right. That is all we need to know about the cockpit until we are ready to take-off.

Captain Jack takes a look out of his cockpit window. He sees that the fuel tanker has finished loading fuel which is called uplifting for an aircraft. He notices that the lorry carrying all the food and drinks for the flight has also left. This means that Suki and her crew will be making sure that it is all safely stored away before take-off.

Finally he sees the "honey-wagon" leaving. This is a strange name for a lorry. It has a large tank on the back of it. But it has a very important job to do after each flight. All the waste material that goes down the toilets ends up in a tank on board the aircraft and that has to be emptied after each flight. And that is the job of the honey-wagon.

Jack has to smile because he knows that a lot of people still think that when you flush a toilet in the air, it all goes out of the aircraft and lands on the ground. He knows that this is just not true.

But now the time is approaching their departure time and he and Alisha will soon have to start the engines.

Captain Jack's Questions

"Which seat does Captain Jack sit on in the cockpit?"

"What does PFD stand for?"

"If the horizon bar on the PFD goes down, what is the aircraft doing?"

"Which colour of clouds on the navigation screen shows very bad weather?"

"Which screen shows what the engines are doing?"

"What is the old name for the control column?"

"If the control column is moved to the left, what will the aircraft do?"

"What is carried in the honey-wagon?"

Jet Engines

Most big airliners have jet engines and not propellers to power them. The first jet engine was invented by a British engineer called Sir Frank Whittle in 1937. However the first jet aircraft was German – the Heinkel 178 and was a single seater. But it was Britain who built the first jet airliner in 1949. It was called the Comet 4. The first regular jet flights across the Atlantic Ocean began in 1958.

Turbine Blades of a Jet Engine

If you look closely at a modern jet engine, you will see that it is bigger at the front than at the back. And if you are able to look at the front of one you will see lots of blades called turbine blades rotating around a central core.

When the engine is operating, the turbine blades spin very quickly and suck in lots of air. This air is then crushed smaller by what is called a compressor. This happens a couple of times before the very compressed air is introduced into the combustion chamber where it is mixed with burning fuel.

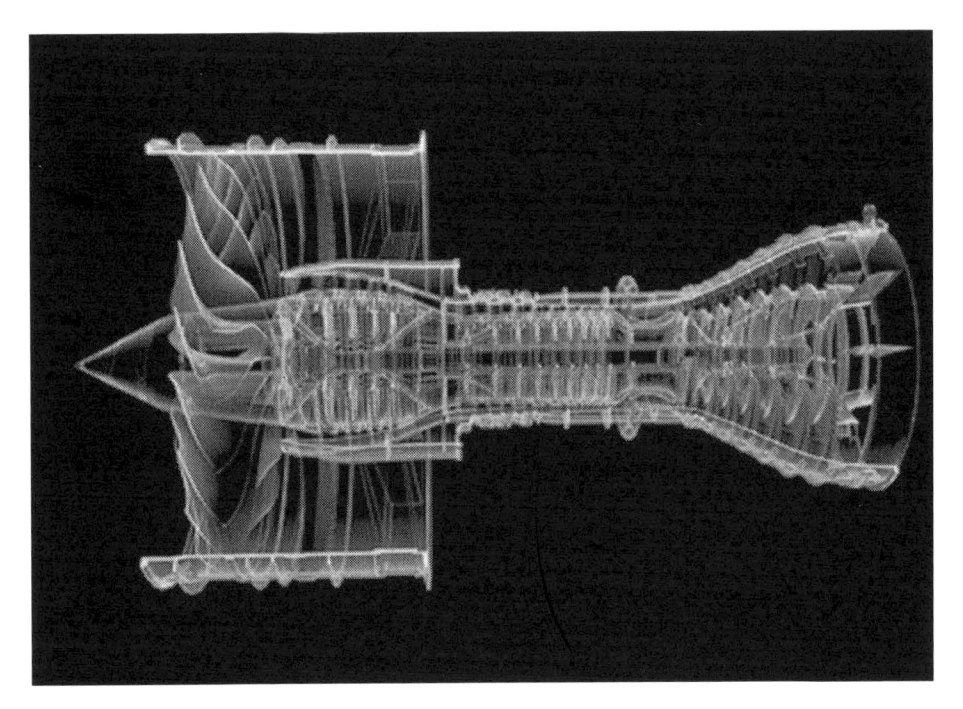

Cut-Away Diagram of a Jet Engine

This causes the gas mixture to suddenly expand enormously and very quickly. The gas is then pushed out of the engine exhaust at the rear of the engine at very great speed. This causes an opposite reaction which pushes the aircraft forwards. The reason for this comes from a famous scientist called Sir Isaac Newton who said in his Third Law of Motion: "To every action (the exhaust gases being pushed backwards) there is an equal and opposite reaction (the plane moving forwards)."

Jet engines can be very dangerous to stand next to when they are running. If somebody forgets and stands in front of the engine, they could be sucked into it. And if they stand behind the exhaust, the hot gases could easily burn them. So the ground engineers at airports are always very careful. And Captain Jack makes a last check to see that all is clear before he is ready to start the engines.

Captain Jack's Questions

"Who invented the jet engine?"

"What was the first jet airliner called?"

"In what engine chamber is air mixed with burning fuel?"

"Finish this sentence, "To every action there is an...""

"Who discovered the Third Law of Motion?"

Engine Start

The airliner is now ready. All the passengers are aboard and safely strapped into their seats. Suki and her team have also closed the aircraft doors. In the cockpit, all the pre-start checklists have been completed and Captain Jack has given Alisha a final briefing to cover the take-off.

Push Back Truck in Action

She now uses the radio to talk to the Ground part of Air Traffic Control and requests a "Push-Back." This means that a low but powerful truck will attach itself to the nose wheel of the aircraft. The driver will then slowly drive his truck forwards, thereby pushing the jet backwards away from the terminal building.

As the aircraft is being pushed back, it is time to start the engines. Aircraft engines are numbered 1, 2, 3 and 4 from left to right as seen from the cockpit. On Captain Jack's plane there are two engines. It is normal practice to start the engines in reverse order. So engine number 2 under the right wing will be the first.

Engine Start Panel

It is not too difficult to start a jet engine. Captain Jack first selects the Engine Start switch and rotates it to the Ignition Start position. At this point, the passengers may notice a reduction in the noise of the air conditioning. This is because all of the air is now being diverted to power up the high pressure compressor in the engine.

Next Captain Jack turns on the Fuel Master switch to engine number 2. Fuel will now flow into the combustion chamber and is mixed with the compressed air. The fuel and air mixture is then ignited by a set of igniters in the combustion chamber. The engine starts and is soon running under its own power. Jack will now go through the same procedure for engine number 1.

By the time the truck has finished pushing the plane into position and unhooking itself from the airliner nose wheel, both of the engines are working and are set to idle power. Alisha now radios air traffic control again and requests permission for them to taxi out to the runway. They give their permission and Captain Jack pushes the throttles forwards a little bit. The engine noise increases and soon they are taxiing.

Captain Jack's Questions

"Is engine number 1 on the left or right side of the aircraft?"

"Which position does the engine start switch go to?"

"What do the engines do when you move the throttles forward?"

Taxi

Taxiing an aircraft is in some ways similar to driving a car, except that it is a lot bigger. So Captain Jack has to obey a number of "rules of the road" as he taxies the airliner to the runway.

There is a set route for him to follow and he has to be alert for any other aircraft and vehicles that may also be moving around the airport apron and taxiways. Large airports are very busy, not just with other aircraft but with all the ground vehicles looking after the planes.

Airliner Taxiing out to the Runway

He must also listen out in case air traffic control tells him to halt and wait for another aircraft to pass. There is a speed limit when taxiing a plane and it is about 22 miles per hour.

Air Traffic Control Tower

There are a number of items to be checked whilst taxiing. One of these is lowering the flaps both at the front and rear of the wings. These have the effect of increasing the area of the wings and therefore will give the aircraft more lift. There are disadvantages to using flaps such as increased drag but these factors are outweighed by the advantages when taking-off and on landing.

Both Jack and Alisha have separate brakes which can be activated by pressing down on the tops of their rudder pedals. They now test them to make sure they are working correctly. However, as we shall see later, this is not the main method of slowing down an aircraft when landing.

When taxiing, Jack can either steer the aircraft using his rudder pedals or by using a small steering wheel to one side of him. This operates the nose-wheel. He has to be very careful as it is easy to cause a skid. This is especially important when Jack is steering the airliner in a turn.

Meanwhile Alisha is going through the Before Take-Off checklist. She looks up and sees they have reached the Holding Point of the runway they will be using to take-off today. Different runways are used depending on which way the wind is blowing. However there is another aircraft in front of them which is moving onto the runway and lining up ready for take-off.

Jack stops the plane at the holding point and Alisha radios air traffic control to tell them they are holding and are ready to line-up. When the other aircraft has safely taken-off, the controller tells Alisha that they have permission to line-up.

After every instruction, Alisha has to repeat it so that the controller is happy the message has been received and understood correctly.

Captain Jack now moves the aircraft onto the runway and positions it on the centre line. They now wait for the controller to give them permission to take-off. When it comes, Alisha reads back the permission and they are ready to take-off.

Captain Jack's Questions

"What is the speed limit for taxiing aircraft?"

"What do the wing flaps do?"

"Which two ways can you steer an aircraft when taxiing?"

"Name the position you wait at to enter the runway?"

Take-Off and Climb

Captain Jack makes one final check to see if there is a crosswind. But it is light and will pose no problem to them. An aircraft will always take-off and land into the wind if it can as it makes both the take-off and landing run shorter.

Engine Throttles (centre)

Jack pushes the two throttle levers forwards and the engine noise begins to increase. He stops at about 30% of maximum power for a few moments to make sure both engines are running smoothly. When he is satisfied they are working normally, he pushes the throttles forwards to 90% of maximum power and then releases the brakes.

The airliner begins to accelerate and the passengers feel themselves being pushed gently back into their seats. Faster and faster it accelerates. Captain Jack keeps the aircraft on the centre line by using his rudder pedals to steer it. At 80 knots or nautical miles per hour, Jack and Alisha check that their airspeed indicators are in agreement. If they were different, Jack would stop the aircraft. But they are reading the same so the take-off run continues.

The throttles are still set at 90% and this is known as Flexible/Maximum Continuous Thrust or FLX MCT. Alisha checks the thrust setting and confirms "Thrust Set."

The next call Alisha makes to Jack is "V1". This means that the aircraft can no longer stop before the runway finishes, so they are now committed to take-off. In answer to this, Captain Jack removes his right hand from the throttles.

The next critical speed Alisha is looking out for is known as Vr. This is the speed at which Jack can rotate the aircraft and allow it to take-off. When he hears the call he gently eases back on the control column. The nose of the airliner rises and the next moment the wheels leave the ground and they are flying.

Rotate and Take-Off

Alisha is now looking for another critical speed. This one is called V2 and it is the aircraft safety speed which means the minimum speed it needs to maintain a climb. However, pilots always add a bit extra to this figure. So Alisha calls out V2 + 10 knots. Captain Jack now calls

"Gear Up" which is the command to raise the undercarriage. Alisha grabs hold of the undercarriage lever and moves it upwards. Immediately three green lights on the instrument panel turn to red. This tells the pilots that the undercarriage is moving. When all the wheels are safely stored and the hatches have closed, the three red lights go out.

Undercarriage is being Retracted

Captain Jack's Questions

"In which wind direction does a plane take-off and land?"

"What does the term V1 mean?"

"What colour are the three lights when the undercarriage is moving?"

Climbing to Cruising Altitude

It is not unusual to put an aircraft onto Autopilot soon after take-off. But many pilots including Captain Jack prefer to fly the airliner manually to about 10,000 feet before selecting "George", the nickname given to all autopilot systems.

As the aircraft gains height there is still plenty to do in the cockpit. The throttles are reduced to a mark that says CLM. This is the setting for Climb Power and this also brings the Auto-Thrust into operation. The auto-thrust will ensure that both engines will run at the right power until the plane reaches cruising altitude.

The aircraft is now passing through a height of 4,000 feet. Captain Jack orders the flaps to be raised. This happens in stages. When Jack wants the final stage raised he calls for "Flaps Zero." Alisha is operating the flap lever and when they are fully raised she confirms "Flaps are Zero." Alisha now goes through the After Take-Off checklist.

During the climb Alisha also has to change radio frequency in order to talk to other parts of the air traffic control system. She will continue to do this as the plane flies over different countries on its way to its destination of Athens.

Airliner Climbing to Cruise Altitude

Air traffic control need to know the identity of any particular aircraft on their radar screens. So they give each plane a four number code to put into an instrument called a Transponder. Alisha keys in the four number code she has been given and then presses a button entitled "Squawk

Ident". This has the effect of momentarily lighting up their aircraft on the radar screen making it easy for the controller to identify their plane. It also tells the controller the height they are flying at.

Transponder codes can also be used to tell air traffic control of situations aboard the aircraft without using the radio. These are usually associated with problems arising which are very rare. There are three such codes and all Jack or Alisha need to do is key-in the appropriate code and the controller will know the type of problem on board.

For example, if a passenger was interfering with a flight, the crew would squawk 7500. If the aircraft's radio failed they could key in 7600. Lastly if there was an emergency on board like the sort you would send a Mayday signal, then you would input 7700 into the transponder.

Captain Jack has now put the aircraft on autopilot and is approaching its cruising altitude. Today it is 36,000 feet or Flight Level 360 as pilots would say. With 1,000 feet to go, Captain Jack calls out "One to Go." When cruising level is reached the autopilot reduces the engine thrust from CLM (climb) to Altitude Cruise (ALT CRZ).

Captain Jack's Questions

"What is the nickname given to autopilots?"

"What does CL stand for on the throttle control?"

"How many numbers are there in a transponder code?"

"What is the transponder code for a radio failure?"

"What is the transponder code for an emergency or Mayday?"

"What flight level is 34,000 feet?"

On-Route Cruising

At this point of the flight, termed "Top of Climb" we will leave Jack and Alisha to their duties and check on Suki and her cabin crew. They will soon be serving refreshments and a meal as the flight time to Athens is about four hours.

The seatbelt sign has been switched off. This usually means that most of the passengers will undo their seatbelts completely. Suki is right to believe that this is not a good idea. Even though Captain Jack and Alisha can see if there is any bad weather ahead of them, it is possible to suddenly encounter turbulence without any warning. This type of weather condition is known as a CAT. But don't worry it doesn't mean that there is a cat floating in the air. The term stands for "Clear Air Turbulence" and although not very common, it is always a good idea to keep your seatbelt lightly fastened.

Depending on the length of the flight, Jack and Alisha will also be offered refreshments and a meal. Many people have heard that the pilots never eat the same meals in case they should get food poisoning. This is true and there is always a choice of meals so Jack and Alisha never eat the same food on a flight.

We will leave Suki and her team to get on with their work and re-join Jack and Alisha in the cockpit. The cruise part of the flight is usually slightly less busy than take-off and landing, but there is still plenty to do including checking all the various aircraft systems are functioning correctly. Let's take a look at some of those now.

Captain Jack's Questions

"What is the flying time roughly from London to Athens?"

"What does CAT stand for?"

"Why should you keep your seatbelt loosely fastened?"

"Why do pilots never eat the same food?"

Pressurisation and Air Conditioning

All airliners flying above 10,000 feet or Flight Level 100 are pressurised. This is very important because at 36,000 feet which is the cruising level of our flight, the air temperature outside is close to minus 60 degrees Celsius. In addition to this, the pressure outside the aircraft is so low and containing so little oxygen, you would not be able to breathe.

Therefore it is important that the inside of the aircraft is pressurised so that it feels comfortable and you can breathe easily just like being on the ground. But it is not exactly the same as being on the ground at sea level. If it was then the difference in pressure would be very big and require that the aircraft walls to be made much thicker. This would make the plane heavier and therefore it would need more fuel and be more expensive to fly.

To get over this problem, the aircraft is pressurised to a height of about 6,000 feet. The pressure difference between the inside and outside of the aircraft is now reduced to 30,000 feet rather than 36,000 feet. The pressure inside the aircraft is the same as you would feel if you stood on top of a 6,000 foot mountain. And at this height you would not notice the reduction in oxygen pressure and it would feel normal to you.

Airliners are Pressurised to about 6,000 feet

However it does have one interesting effect. Because the air pressure is lower, it means that water will boil at a lower temperature. Normally water boils at 100 degrees Celsius but at 6,000 feet it will boil at about 90 degrees Celsius. Now if you are drinking a cup of tea, it tastes better if the water is very hot. Coffee tastes fine if it is a few degrees cooler. So you can say that coffee tastes better in an airliner than tea.

The temperature of the air inside the aircraft cabin is kept at a comfortably warm level by bleeding off some of the hot air produced by the engines. But because the air is very hot and contains some fumes, it must first be cooled and filtered before it is piped into the cabin for the passengers to breathe.

It is not only the cabin which is kept warm. At least one of the holds will be warm and fed fresh air. This is because aircraft often carry live animals on their flights. They are kept in the hold and have their own special travelling containers from which they can drink water and eat.

There is another interesting fact about aircraft pressurisation. Did you know that during a flight, the passenger doors remain unlocked? This might sound a bit worrying at first. What would happen if somebody accidently pulled on the door handle? Well there is no need to worry.

All passenger doors first have to be pulled inwards before they can be opened outwards. This means that to open a door in flight, you first have to overcome the air pressure difference keeping the door closed. This pressure is so great that you would have to have the strength of Superman to open it. So you are perfectly safe.

Captain Jack's Questions

"What roughly is the outside temperature at 36,000 feet?"

"To what height are aircraft cabins pressurised to?"

"At what temperature does water boil in a pressurised aircraft?"

"Why will one cargo hold be heated?"

"Why is it impossible to open a passenger door during a flight?"

Fuel Management

If you remember we talked about fuel when the aircraft was on the ground. We also saw that the fuel is loaded or uplifted into the fuel tanks which are located in the wings. But if you thought that was the end of the story, you would be wrong. The fuel load plays another important role other than just powering the engines.

Throughout a flight, the fuel load has to be managed and this means that it must be continuously moved around the different tanks in the wings. This is because as the fuel is burnt off in the engines, the weight reduces and this can affect the balance or "Centre of Gravity" of the aircraft. This can be illustrated when the plane taxies out to the runway, takes off and then climbs to cruising height.

On the ground the fuel is pumped to those tanks which are closest to the fuselage. If this didn't happen then the tips of the wings would bend downwards and put a lot of strain on them. The part of the wing that is close to the fuselage is stronger than the ends so it is sensible to fill those tanks when taxiing and taking off.

However when the aircraft takes off, the lift generated in the wings has the effect of bending the wing tips upwards. So to compensate, fuel is pumped from the inner tanks to the outer tanks to balance the extra lift with the increased weight.

Movement of the fuel continues throughout a flight, keeping the aircraft in balance. Luckily for Captain Jack and Alisha there is a computer which does all of this for them. But part of their duties is to monitor the fuel to make sure the computer is doing the job correctly. Although lots of the systems are automatic and run by computers, the task of the pilots is to make sure everything is working as it should. Therefore the pilots are always in charge of the aircraft.

This is a good time to consider a certain type of emergency. All emergencies are very rare and all pilots practice getting out of them on a regular basis in flight simulators. In this particular case let's imagine that there is a technical problem soon after the aircraft has taken off and it means that Captain Jack and Alisha must return to the airport and land so the problem can be fixed. Now it is usual for airliners to be able to take-off with a heavier weight than they can land with. Aircraft will always land lighter because the fuel has been burnt off. But in the case of needing to land just after a take-off, this will give Captain Jack an additional problem.

But not to worry, there is a plan to solve this problem. First of all it is possible to land a very heavy aircraft safely. The problem arises because it could overstress certain parts of the airframe. So the answer is to dump some of the fuel before landing with a much lighter aircraft.

Captain Jack would normally fly the plane to an uninhabited area such as the ocean and then fly a circuit pattern. He can now safely jettison some of the fuel he does not need. At the end of each wingtip there is a small hose from which the fuel will be jettisoned. To do this, all Captain Jack has to do is tell the computer what weight he wants to land with and press the jettison button. The computer does the rest and soon Captain Jack can return to the airport and make a safe landing.

Captain Jack's Questions

"When taxiing, where is the fuel pumped to?"

"Where do pilots practice emergencies?"

"Where is the hose to jettison fuel located?"

Electrical System

As well as providing the aircraft's lighting, there are many systems which depend on an electricity supply to power them up. To achieve this there are a number of electrical generators on board. These are powered by the aircraft engines.

The instruments and systems on board use electricity in its "Direct Current" or DC form. However the generators produce "Alternating Current" or AC which needs to be converted using equipment called Rectifiers. Captain Jack and Alisha will monitor these generators to make sure all their instruments have enough power.

But what would happen if on some rare occasion something unusual happened and all the generators failed? Well just like so many other systems on board there are back-up supplies ready to take over. For example each generator has a back-up battery attached to it. There is also the Auxiliary Power Unit or APU available. This sits in the tail of the aircraft and is often used to supply power when the plane is on the ground and before engine start-up.

However what would happen if all these back-up systems failed as well? In that case Jack and Alisha would release the RAT. Don't worry it's not a big furry rodent. In fact RAT stands for "Ram Air Turbine". It basically consists of a propeller which can be lowered down under the aircraft. The force of the wind turns the propeller and this generates power. It can only produce about 10% of the power required but this is enough for Jack and Alisha to fly and land the aircraft safely.

Captain Jack's Questions

"What powers the electrical generators?"

"Do aircraft systems use direct current or alternating current?"

"What does APU stand for?"

"Where in the aircraft can you find the APU?"

"What is the RAT?"

"How much power can a RAT supply to an aircraft?"

Fire Protection Systems

One of the biggest fears amongst passengers is what would happen if a fire broke out during a flight? Smoking is no longer allowed in an aircraft which is a very good thing. But if a passenger thinks that they can sneak into one of the toilets and have a smoke, then they are going to be in for a big surprise.

Each toilet is fitted with a fire and a smoke alarm which tells both the pilots and the cabin crew that there is something wrong. If there was a fire in the cabin then there are plenty of fire extinguishers on board for Suki and her crew to put it out.

However, in the very rare event of a fire, it can often be in the engines. But don't worry because Jack and Alisha have a number of procedures which will put the fire out. And like everything else, they practice them in the flight simulator on a regular basis, so they are always ready.

Let's show you how Captain Jack and Alisha would tackle a fire in one of the engines. First of all they would be alerted in the cockpit by both visual and audio alarms. There is a "Fire Control Panel" which will tell them where the fire is located. The operation to put an engine fire out is called an "Isolate and Extinguish" procedure.

Once the engine on fire is identified, the throttle to that engine is pulled back. This is followed by switching off the "Master" switch to that engine. Captain Jack and Alisha will then check the Fire Control Panel. They will see a large red button illuminated. There are two words printed on the button – "Fire Push". They immediately press the button.

Straight away the fuel to that engine is cut-off along with all electrics and hydraulics. These actions have now isolated the engine. Now it is time to put the fire out. Each engine has two separate fire extinguisher systems. They are called "Agent 1" and "Agent 2".

The button controlling Agent 1 is pressed and this sets off a fire extinguisher located inside the engine compartment. The crew now wait for 30 seconds to confirm that the fire has gone out. If this is not the case, then Agent 2 is activated. This empties another extinguisher into the engine compartment. It is very unlikely a fire would survive two fire extinguishers.

If a fire should start in one of the cargo holds, Jack and Alisha would first cut-off the air supply to that compartment to starve the fire of oxygen. They would then operate the fire extinguisher system in that hold to make sure the fire had gone out. There is a separate system for each cargo hold.

So even though a fire is a serious but rare event, the pilots can deal with the problem quickly and effectively. And if you are wondering what happens because one of the two engines has now been stopped, once again, don't worry. Modern two engine airliners can quite easily fly on one engine.

We have looked at the different systems on board and talked about how to deal with some emergencies. But these of course rarely happen on a flight. What does happen on every flight is that Captain Jack and Alisha have to navigate the aircraft and communicate with the ground. So that is what we shall look at next.

Captain Jack's Questions

"What two types of alarm are located in aircraft toilets?"

"What is the procedure for putting out an engine fire called?"

"What two words are on the big red button?"

"What are the two engine fire extinguisher systems called?"

"How long must you wait to see if the engine fire has gone out?"

"What is the first thing to do with a cargo hold fire?"

Navigation

Many years ago, pilots had paper charts and old radio beacons to navigate by. Although pilots still learn to navigate using these methods during their training, these days navigation is a lot more sophisticated. The present system is known as the "Inertial Reference System" or IRS and it uses laser guided gyros to tell them where they are and where they are going.

It is similar to the GPS system you find in many motor cars except the IRS is much more accurate. In fact it is so accurate that the distances between aircraft have been able to be reduced. And if the aircraft and airport have the correct equipment installed, a plane can land without the pilot interfering. This might be the case if the visibility was very bad. In a few years' time this might become very common.

Earlier we saw the Navigation Display or ND in the cockpit and we also know that Jack and Alisha have one each. Before the flight started Captain Jack and Alisha would have programmed their route into the navigation computer by using their Multi-Functional Displays.

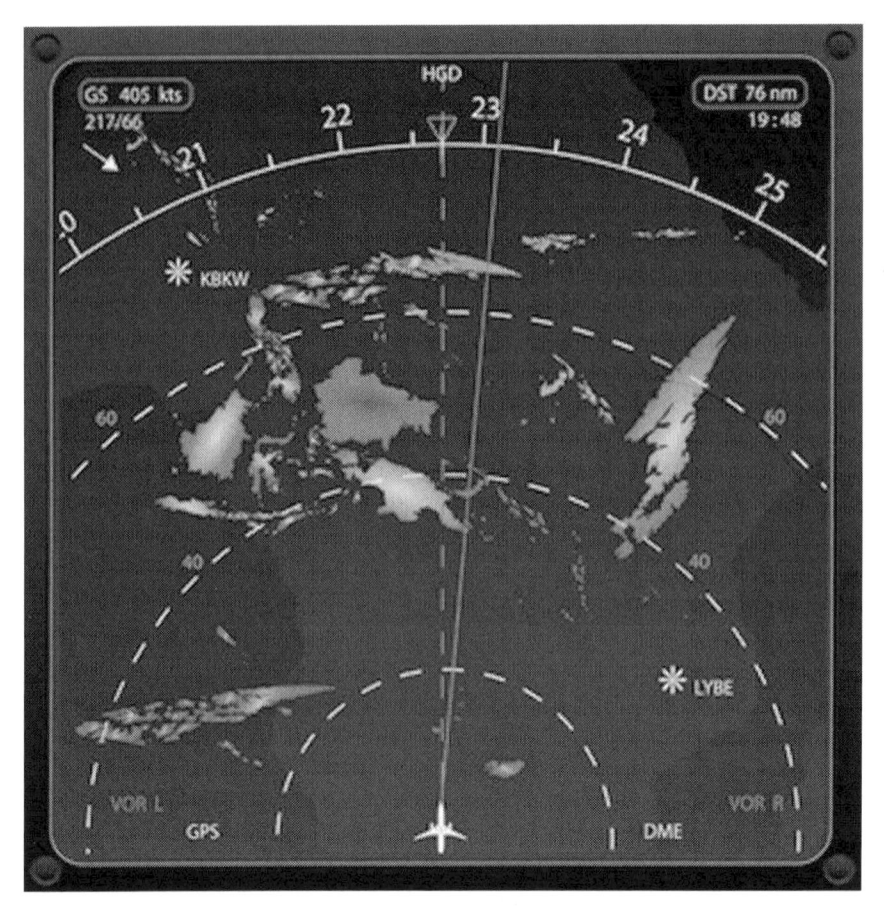

Navigation Display shows the Weather Ahead

The navigation display can show a number of different screens but the main one is the route they will be flying. And as we learned earlier, Jack and Alisha can also overlay the weather ahead of them. If it looks bad they can change their route and fly around or over it.

The planned route will also contain the altitude the plane will fly at. In this flight we know it is 36,000 feet. But this is likely to change during the flight. As the fuel is burnt off, the aircraft becomes lighter and therefore it will be more efficient to fly a bit higher. There are set altitudes for aircraft to fly at and air traffic control can give permission to change altitude.

After about two hours into the flight Alisha calls the local controller and asks if they can climb to a higher altitude. The controller checks the radar screen to make sure there is no other plane close by and when they are satisfied, they give Jack and Alisha permission to climb to 38,000 feet.

As the aircraft passes overhead different countries, then new air traffic control centres take over. It is Alisha's job as the pilot not flying (PNF) to talk to each of the centres as they reach them. This will mean re-tuning the radio to a new frequency.

Sometimes they might be in contact with a controller for a long time; for example flying across an ocean. At other times, say over Europe, they might have to change frequency quite often.

But since we are talking about the radio let's take a closer look at aircraft communications.

Captain Jack's Questions

"What does IRS stand for in navigation?"

"What does an IRS use to calculate the aircraft's position?"

"Why might an aircraft climb higher during a flight?"

"What does PNF stand for?"

Communications

Although most communications still involve talking directly to a controller on the ground, pilots are increasingly using "Data Links". This means that messages are typed out and sent directly to the pilot or to the ground. The advantage of this is that there is less of a chance of misinterpreting any message. There is of course a term for this and it is a bit of a mouthful. It is called "Controller Pilot Data Link Communication" or CPDLC.

This might sound a bit like texting and you would not be far wrong. To make things even easier for pilots, many of the messages have been standardised and kept on file within the computer. Therefore, for many messages, all Alisha needs to do is select the message she wants and press "Send".

Another advantage of this system is that sometimes a number of different aircraft all want to talk to the same controller at the same time. This can happen where a number of airways converge on each other. An "Airway" can be thought of as a road for aircraft. They must stay on the road until a controller gives them permission to leave it. Of course a pilot can change height and course if there is a sudden emergency but they will inform the controller as soon as they can.

Pilots Wear Lightweight Headsets to Communicate

These new systems were first tested out over the Pacific Ocean. There are very few places to locate radio masts and since normal VHF radio has a range of about 250 nautical miles at normal cruising altitudes, then a new method had to be found. The first attempt was to use High Frequency or HF radio which has a greater range. But that system has limitations, so the digital link system became a favourite.

However there is one disadvantage. Whilst it is very efficient over oceans, it can be a bit slow sending and receiving messages in areas where the airspace is congested, for example over Europe. Many pilots still prefer to talk directly to controllers under such conditions.

We have now covered all of the systems that Captain Jack and Alisha will be monitoring during their flight to Athens. But time is moving on and it will soon be time to prepare to descend and land at Athens airport.

Captain Jack's Questions

"What does CPDLC stand for?"

"What do pilots call a route which they fly along just like a car on a road?"

"At 36,000 feet what is the normal range of a VHF radio in nautical miles?"

"What is the disadvantage of using data link messages?"

Descent

As the cruise part of the flight is nearing an end, Suki and her team are making sure all the meal and drink services have been cleared away. In the cockpit the computer is calculating where the best point to begin to descend is. This point is known as the "Top of Descent" mark.

At Top of Descent the Engines are Throttled Back

When the computer has decided this, a downward pointing arrow appears on the navigation display telling

Jack and Alisha how long they have before beginning their descent.

Captain Jack now briefs Alisha about the flight plan which covers the descent and landing. It is similar to the take-off briefing and will include such items as the proposed approach to the airport, the radio direction beacons they will use to guide them and what is called the "Go-Around" procedure.

This is the route taken by pilots if for some reason they are unable to land. The procedure is a standard one for each airport and is published on the "Approach Plate" for that particular airport. An approach plate is a small chart showing the route into an airport and where to fly if you cannot land.

Captain Jack and Alisha have also obtained the latest weather at their destination airport. They check it carefully to make sure it is still safe to land. Luckily there are no problems. It says there are scattered clouds at 3,000 feet and only a light northerly wind. This will pose no problems for the pilots.

Captain Jack next makes a call to the passengers on the intercom to update them on the time of landing and the weather conditions they can expect. Whilst he is doing this, Alisha has started going through the "Descent" checklist.

Descending – the Approach Plate is on the Right

As the aircraft reaches the top of descent mark, Alisha asks the air traffic controller for permission to begin their descent. Permission is granted and Captain Jack pulls the throttles back and the aircraft begins a controlled glide down. There is a best rate of descent and the computer makes sure that the aircraft maintains this. Once again,

Jack and Alisha will be checking the flight instruments to make sure everything is going to plan.

For every major airport there is a set route for departing and another for arriving. The departure is called a SID which stands for "Standard Instrument Departure" whilst the arriving procedure is called a STAR. This stands for "Standard Terminal Arrival Route". Captain Jack and Alisha will be following the STAR procedure as shown on their Approach Plates.

The aircraft is descending in stages. This means that Jack and Alisha can only descend to the altitude given to them by the air traffic controller. However it is usual to be cleared to a new lower level before you reach the one before so that the descent is continuous. If a clearance is not received then Jack and Alisha must stay at their last cleared altitude until the controller gives them permission to descend to a lower level.

The route the aircraft is taking is to follow a line of selected radio beacons. At each beacon the plane will change heading if necessary and fly directly to the next beacon in line. The normal rate of descent for an airliner is about 2,500 feet per minute. But if required, this can be increased to about 5,000 feet per minute using air brakes.

Okay, the aircraft is now passing through 10,000 feet and Captain Jack calls for the next checklist. One of the items listed is for the seatbelt signs to be switched on. Suki and her team start to get all the passengers back to their seats and to fasten their seatbelts. In the cockpit, Alisha switches on the bright landing lights which point forwards from the aircraft. They are a bit like a car's headlights only much bigger and more powerful.

The altimeter will soon be reset to show the height of the aircraft above sea-level. This is known as the QNH setting. Jack and Alisha tick off each item on the "Landing Checklist" until they arrive at the flap settings. The list is now halted until it is time to begin lowering the flaps.

When deployed, the flaps enable the aircraft to land at a slower speed. They are lowered in stages; Flaps 1, 2, 3… So when the time arrives, Captain Jack calls for "Flaps 1." Alisha moves the flap lever to configuration 1 which is marked on the flap control as Config 1. The flaps roll out at the front and rear edges of the wings until they reach their number 1 position. The front edge of the wing is called its Leading Edge and the rear edge is termed the Trailing Edge. The aircraft is now approaching the final stages before landing.

Captain Jack's Questions

"What is the point where the plane begins to descend called?"

"What is the small chart showing how to land at each airport called?"

"What does SID stand for?"

"What does STAR stand for?"

"What is the normal descent rate for an airliner?"

"What three letter altimeter setting shows height above sea-level?"

"What is the front edge of a wing called?"

"What is the rear edge of a wing called?"

Landing

Up until this stage, Captain Jack has kept the autopilot flying the aircraft. However, he and Alisha have been monitoring and cross-checking all the information to make sure the systems are working properly.

The next beacon in line is called the "Initial Approach Fix" or IAF. When the aircraft passes over it at a specific height, it will turn in accordance with the STAR procedure. At some airports there might be a number of beacons to fly over but on this flight the IAF directs us onto the Final Approach to the landing runway.

The controller responsible for all the landing aircraft gives Jack and Alisha permission to land. Alisha repeats the permission back to the controller in order to show that the message has been received and understood.

The aircraft is heading towards another beacon. This one is called the "Final Approach Fix" or FAF. In this particular airport procedure, the beacon will direct the aircraft onto the ILS or "Instrument Landing System".

The ILS is a very accurate way of guiding an aircraft down onto the runway. Once it has been intercepted or "captured" as pilots say, a glideslope appears on the Primary Flight Display in front of each pilot. By aligning the aircraft up with the glideslope and faithfully following it down, it will lead the plane to a safe landing.

So with the Instrument Landing System captured, Captain Jack decides to take over manual control of the aircraft and fly it down to a landing himself. He presses the autopilot disconnect button. This is a small control located on his control column. The autopilot is immediately disconnected and Jack is now flying the plane.

Aircraft Approaching to Land

He calls for "Flaps 2" and Alisha moves the flap lever to the next mark. The speed of the aircraft drops and Jack calls for the undercarriage to be lowered ready for landing.

Alisha pulls out the undercarriage lever and moves it to the down position. The three red lights come on again to show that the wheels are in transit. Once they are down and locked, the red lights turn to green. Alisha calls out "Three Greens."

Captain Jack now calls for "Flaps 3." The aircraft continues to descend towards the runway. Jack continuously checks that he is still on the glideslope. He then calls for "Full Flaps" and Alisha lowers the flap lever to its full deployment mark. She can now finish off the landing checklist.

The aircraft reaches its "Decision Height". This is the point at which Captain Jack has to confirm he can see the runway and is happy to continue the approach to land.

If he could not see the runway or was not happy about something, then he would abort the landing and initiate the "Go-Around" procedure before making a second attempt to land. However he is happy and continues the approach.

Full Flaps Deployed behind the Wings

At 300 feet above the ground, Captain Jack and Alisha hear an artificial voice calling out "300." This is the voice of the Radio Altimeter which is a very accurate piece of equipment which tells the pilots exactly how high they are above the ground. From 300 feet, it will call out every 100 feet until it reaches 50 feet. Then it will call out every 10 feet.

At 50 feet, Captain Jack eases the control column back. This raises the aircraft's nose which has the effect of slowing their rate of descent. It also positions the main undercarriage wheels so that they will be the first to meet the runway on landing.

Then Jack and Alisha hear the same voice call "Retard." This tells Jack that he must now pull the throttles back to the "Idle" position. The engines will now be at minimum power. Jack holds the aircraft off just above the runway and allows it to gently sink the last couple of feet onto the runway. He then slowly lowers the nose of the aircraft until the nose-wheel is in contact with the runway. The aircraft is now safely on the runway.

Main Undercarriage Wheels Touch First

Speed brakes deploy automatically in order to cut any lift left in the wings. After all, if you've just landed, the last thing you want to do is take-off again by mistake. This also has the effect of slowing the aircraft. The level of braking can be set in the computer before landing. But there is another form of braking which is much more effective.

All passengers are aware that just after landing, there is usually a big increase in engine noise. This is due to the "Reverse Thrust" being used. By moving the throttles further back, the engines are able to reverse the direction of their thrust which has a strong effect on slowing the aircraft down quickly.

When the plane is at a slow speed, the reverse thrust is disconnected and normal braking can take over. Captain Jack steers the aircraft off the runway and onto one of the taxiways. He has already been told which stand they will be parking at and the taxi route he should take to arrive there.

Alisha is going through the "After Landing" checklist. The flaps are recovered back into the wings and the auxiliary power unit is switched back on to provide power once the engines are cut. She also turns off all non-essential items. She looks up and sees them approaching their designated parking stand. The flight is almost over for the crew.

Captain Jack's Questions

"What does IAF stand for?"

"Why does Alisha repeat back messages from the controller?"

"What does FAF stand for?"

"What is the Instrument Landing System?"

"Where is the autopilot disconnect button located?"

"What colour are the three lights when the undercarriage is down and locked?"

"What call does Captain Jack make to get the flaps fully deployed?"

"What does Captain Jack have to decide at the Decision Height?"

"If he cannot land, what procedure does Captain Jack follow?"

"At what height does the radio altimeter begin giving heights?"

"What term does the radio altimeter use to tell Captain Jack to pull the engines back to idle?"

"Which part of the undercarriage must touch the runway first?"

"What is the main way of slowing an airliner after landing called?"

Arrival and Deplaning

When the aircraft was taxiing out before take-off, Captain Jack made a call to the cabin crew which said "Doors to Automatic." Now as the plane is taxiing in to its parking stand, Jack makes a similar call to the cabin crew; "Doors to Manual."

What this means is that he is ordering the doors to be disarmed. This doesn't mean that they could explode of course. What it does relate to is that if the aircraft had had an emergency and either landed heavily or ditched in the sea, slides would have been deployed at the doors so that the passengers and crew could slide down them to safety. If they had landed in the sea, the slides turn into life-rafts with enough room for everyone.

Captain Jack slowly approaches the parking stand. A ground engineer is on hand to direct him the last few metres. He and Alisha then cut the engines and switch the seatbelt signs off. Any other systems not needed are also switched off. The parking brake has been applied and the ground engineer puts chocks up against the wheels to stop any possible movement. Once the chocks are in place, Jack can release the parking brake.

Alisha completes the "Shut Down" checklist and this gives Captain Jack a chance to get up and say goodbye to some of the passengers as they leave the aircraft. Passengers always seem to like to see one of the pilots and say thanks for the trip.

When the last passenger has deplaned, Jack and the full crew can start to prepare for their return trip to London with a new plane-load of passengers. If it was a long-haul trip meaning they had been flying for longer, Jack and his crew would have stayed the evening in a hotel before flying off on another trip. But Athens is only about four hours flying time away, so they have plenty of time to fly back before they have to take a rest by law.

But since they are returning to London, there is plenty to be done. Alisha has just finished the paperwork for the outward flight. She knows that on the return flight she will be the pilot flying the aircraft and Captain Jack will handle the radio and other systems. But even though Alisha will be flying the aircraft, Captain Jack is still the commander of the flight. But as Jack knows, it will only be a short period before Alisha earns her fourth gold bar and becomes a captain of her own plane.

The Captain and First Officer Share the Flying

You may be reading this book because you want to be an airline pilot in the future. And that is a good thing. It is a great job and one of the best views out of an office window you could possibly get. But it does take hard work and you must be medically fit to fly. But with more and more people taking trips to other countries, it means that pilots will be required for many years to come.

My advice to you is to work hard at school and learn all you can about how planes fly. This book I hope has been the start of your journey to becoming an airline pilot like Captain Jack and First Officer Alisha. Good luck.

Captain Jack's Questions

"What call orders the passenger doors to be disarmed?"

"What does the engineer put against the aircraft wheels to stop them moving when parked at the stand?"

"What is the final checklist called?"

Further Knowledge

Up to this point you have seen how Captain Jack and First Officer Alisha handle a typical flight in a modern airliner; from flight planning to landing and preparing for the next flight. You have also read about some of the not so obvious duties of Suki and her cabin crew and how they are so important if there is a problem with the aircraft.

And so some of you reading this may now really want to become either pilots or cabin crew. In the last section I said that getting a good education in school will help you and passing a medical test is also important. But it is also important that you learn as much as you can about flying before you make your decision to be an aircrew member or not.

The following pages go into flying in a little more detail. No matter whether you decide you want to be a private pilot or a commercial pilot, this is some of the knowledge you will study at a very early stage in your training. Principles of Flight will tell you about how an aircraft flies.

The other piece of advice I will give you is this. No matter where you live there is a good chance that an airfield with a flying club is not too far away. Visit it and ask to talk to a Flying Instructor about the different ways of becoming a pilot. They know what it takes to be a pilot and they can give you help and advice on how to pursue your dream of flying a plane.

Principles of Flight

There are four main forces acting on an aircraft while it is in flight. They are Lift, Weight, Thrust and Drag.

For an aircraft of any size to be able to take-off, it needs to be moving down a runway until the lift generated by the forward motion produces enough lift to leave the runway.

The engine produces the power to move the aircraft but what is the factor that produces the lift? The obvious answer is the wing and you'd be right. But the crucial point is that the wing must be of a certain shape to produce the lift.

This shape is called an airfoil. If you look at an airfoil you will see that the upper surface is more curved than the lower surface. When the air passes over and under the wing as in taking-off, this shape produces different pressures.

Above the wing the air pressure is reduced and below the wing the air pressure is increased. The effect of this is to produce the lift and at the correct speed, the aircraft will take-off and fly.

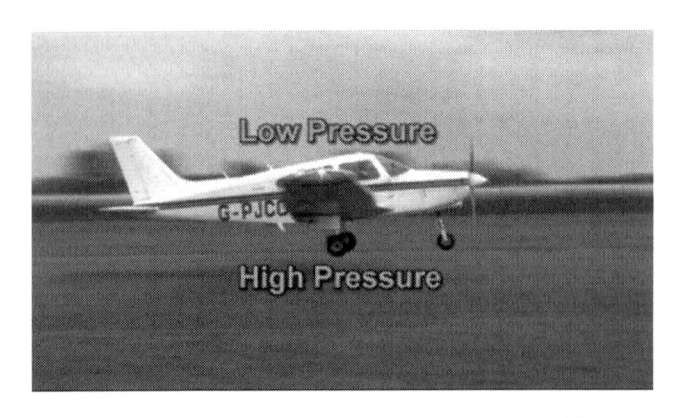

Shape of the Wing produces Lift

When an aircraft is flying, the same four forces are acting on it. If the plane is in straight and level flight, then the forces will balance out each other in the following way.

Lift (acting upwards) is in balance with the aircraft's weight (acting downwards). Thrust (acting forwards) is balanced by drag (acting backwards) which is air friction and acts against the forward motion.

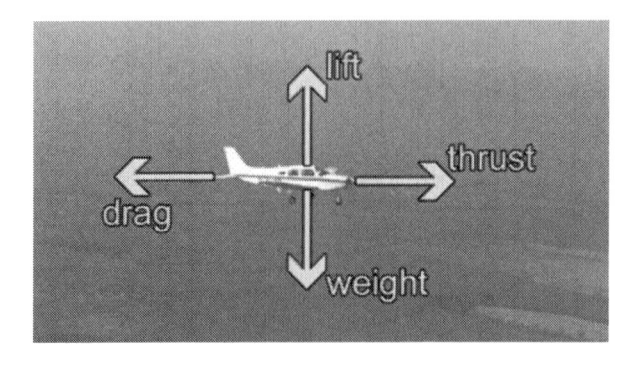

In straight and level flight all forces are in balance

Now if the pilot changes anything such as speed or direction, the forces will go out of balance until the pilot brings them back using the flying controls. And it is the flying controls which we shall look at next.

We read earlier in the book how Jack and Alisha could control the attitude or position of their airliner by moving the control column and rudder pedals. The position or attitude of a plane can be described as three axes passing through the aircraft's centre of gravity. It sounds a little bit complicated but the following pictures will help.

Movement around the Lateral Axis is called Pitching and is controlled by the Elevators (on the horizontal part of the tail) using the Control Column

By moving the control column and rudder pedals the pilot can cause the aircraft to move around these three axes.

The lateral axis can be thought of as a line passing roughly from wing tip to wing tip and by pulling or pushing the control column the plane will pitch up or down. In other words the aircraft will climb or descend.

The longitudinal axis can be imagined as a line running from the front of the aircraft to the rear. When a pilot moves the control column to the left or right, it operates the ailerons located on the trailing edges of the wings.

Movement around the Longitudinal Axis is called Rolling and is controlled by the Ailerons (on the trailing edge of the wings) using the Control Column

The effect is that the plane will roll around that axis and begin to turn in that same direction. Centring the control column will stop the turn from developing further.

Both of the above are controlled using the control column. The final axis is called the normal axis and can be thought of as a line passing vertically through the plane. Once again, this line passes through the aircraft's centre of gravity. This has the effect of what is called yawing the aircraft.

Movement around the Normal Axis is called Yawing and Yaw is controlled by the Rudder (on the vertical part of the tail) using the Rudder Pedals

Yawing is an unusual term but it can be easily imagined as the plane moving left or right with the wings remaining horizontal. Yaw is not controlled with the control column but instead by using the rudder pedals which are operated by the pilot's feet. These are the same pedals that are used to operate one of the braking systems on board the airliner.

There are other ways a pilot can change the attitude of an aircraft. These include changing the throttle setting, deploying flaps, using air brakes or by raising or lowering the undercarriage. This last section has been a little bit more complicated but I have included it to give you an idea of what it will be like when you study flying for real.

Captain Jack's Answers

Flight Plan

"Which room do pilots meet in and check their Flight Plan?"

Answer: Crew Briefing Room

"How many gold stripes does a Captain have?"

Answer: Four

"What things do pilots check on their Flight Plan?"

Answer: Route, altitude, weather and anything that might affect the flight

"What does Burn-Off Fuel mean?"

Answer: The fuel used in climbing and descending an aircraft

Pre-Flight Checks

"Which airline do Captain Jack and Alisha work for?"

Answer: Fast World Airlines

"Where in the aircraft are the main fuel tanks located?"

Answer: In the aircraft's wings

"How fast can fuel be pumped into the fuel tanks?"

Answer: Up to 3,000 litres per minute

"What is Suki's job title?"

Answer: Cabin Services Manager

"How many cabin crew members are on board?"

Answer: Four

"What is the outside inspection of the aircraft called?"

Answer: A Walk-Round

The Cockpit

"Which seat does Captain Jack sit on in the cockpit?"

Answer: Left hand seat

"What does PFD stand for?"

Answer: Primary Flight Display

"If the horizon bar on the PFD goes down, what is the aircraft doing?"

Answer: Climbing

"Which colour of clouds on the navigation screen shows very bad weather?"

Answer: Red

"Which screen shows what the engines are doing?"

Answer: Engine/Warning Display (EWD)

"What is the old name for the control column?"

Answer: Joystick

"If the control column is moved to the left, what will the aircraft do?"

Answer: Will roll to the left and begin to turn in that direction

"What is carried in the honey-wagon?"

Answer: The waste material from the toilets

Jet Engines

"Who invented the jet engine?"

Answer: Sir Frank Whittle

"What was the first jet airliner called?"

Answer: Comet 4

"In what engine chamber is air mixed with burning fuel?"

Answer: Ignition chamber

"Finish this sentence, "To every action there is an...""

Answer: ...equal and opposite reaction

"Who discovered the Third Law of Motion?"

Answer: Sir Isaac Newton

Engine Start

"Is engine number 1 on the left or right side of the aircraft?"

Answer: On the left side from where the pilot is looking

"On starting, which position does the engine start switch go to?"

Answer: Ignition Start

"What do the engines do when you move the throttles forward?"

Answer: They increase in power

Taxi

"What is the speed limit for taxiing aircraft?"

Answer: About 22 miles per hour

"What do the wing flaps do?"

Answer: Increases the surface of the wing to give more lift

"Which two ways can you steer an aircraft when taxiing?"

Answer: Either using the rudder pedals or by a small steering wheel

"Name the position you wait at to enter the runway?"

Answer: Holding Point

Take-Off and Climb

"In which wind direction does a plane take-off and land?"

Answer: Into wind because the aircraft can take-off and land at a slower ground speed

"What does the term V1 mean?"

Answer: The point at which the aircraft must take-off as there is not enough runway left in which to stop safely

"What colour are the three lights when the undercarriage is moving?"

Answer: Red

Climbing to Cruising Altitude

"What is the nickname given to autopilots?"

Answer: George

"What does CL stand for on the throttle control?"

Answer: Climb Power

"How many numbers are there in a transponder code?"

Answer: Four

"What is the transponder code for a radio failure?"

Answer: 7600

What is the transponder code for an emergency or Mayday?"

Answer: 7700

"What flight level is 34,000 feet?"

Answer: Flight Level 340

On-Route Cruising

"What is the flying time roughly from London to Athens?"

Answer: Four hours

"What does CAT stand for?"

Answer: Clear Air Turbulence

"Why should you keep your seatbelt loosely fastened?"

Answer: In case the aircraft experiences turbulence

"Why do pilots never eat the same food?"

Answer: In case they should get food poisoning

Pressurisation and Air Conditioning

"What roughly is the outside temperature at 36,000 feet?"

Answer: Minus 60 degrees Celsius

"To what height are aircraft cabins pressurised to?"

Answer: About 6,000 feet

"At what temperature does water boil in a pressurised aircraft?"

Answer: About 90 degrees Celsius instead of 100 degrees Celsius

"Why will one cargo hold be heated?"

Answer: Animals may be carried in the cargo hold

"Why is it impossible to open a passenger door during a flight?"

Answer: The pressure difference between the outside and inside of the aircraft is too great

Fuel Management

"When taxiing, where is the fuel pumped to?"

Answer: The wing tanks closest to the fuselage

"Where do pilots practice emergencies?"

Answer: In flight simulators

"Where is the hose to jettison fuel located?"

Answer: At the wingtips of the aircraft

Electrical System

"What powers the electrical generators?"

Answer: The aircraft engines

"Do aircraft systems use direct current or alternating current?"

Answer: Direct current

"What does APU stand for?"

Answer: Auxiliary Power Unit

"Where in the aircraft can you find the APU?"

Answer: In the tail of the aircraft

"What is the RAT?"

Answer: Ram Air Turbine

"How much power can a RAT supply to an aircraft?"

Answer: About 10% of total power but enough to fly the plane and land safely

Fire Protection Systems

"What two types of alarm are located in aircraft toilets?"

Answer: Fire alarms and smoke alarms

"What is the procedure for putting out an engine fire called?"

Answer: Isolate and Extinguish

"What two words are on the big red button?"

Answer: Fire Push

"What are the two engine fire extinguisher systems called?"

Answer: Agent 1 and Agent 2

"How long must you wait to see if the engine fire has gone out?"

Answer: 30 seconds

"What is the first thing to do with a cargo hold fire?"

Answer: Turn off the air supply to that hold to starve the fire of oxygen

Navigation

"What does IRS stand for in navigation?"

Answer: Inertial Reference System

"What does an IRS use to calculate the aircraft's position?"

Answer: Laser guided gyros

"Why might an aircraft climb higher during a flight?"

Answer: As it burns off fuel it becomes lighter

"What does PNF stand for?"

Answer: Pilot Not-Flying

Communications

"What does CPDLC stand for?"

Answer: Controller Pilot Data Link Communication

"What do pilots call a route which they fly along just like a car on a road?"

Answer: Airway

"At 36,000 feet what is the normal range of a VHF radio in nautical miles?"

Answer: About 250 nautical miles

"What is the disadvantage of using data link messages?"

Answer: It can take some time before receiving a reply

Descent

"What is the point where the plane begins to descend called?"

Answer: Top of Descent

"What is the small chart showing how to land at each airport called?"

Answer: Approach Plate

"What does SID stand for?"

Answer: Standard Instrument Departure

"What does STAR stand for?"

Answer: Standard Terminal Arrival Route

"What is the normal descent rate for an airliner?"

Answer: About 2,500 feet per minute

"What three letter altimeter setting shows height above sea-level?"

Answer: QNH

"What is the front edge of a wing called?"

Answer: Leading edge

"What is the rear edge of a wing called?"

Answer: Trailing edge

Landing

"What does IAF stand for?"

Answer: Initial Approach Fix

"Why does Alisha repeat back messages from the controller?"

Answer: To make sure the message has been received and understood

"What does FAF stand for?"

Answer: Final Approach Fix

"What is the Instrument Landing System?"

Answer: A very accurate way of guiding an aircraft down to a safe landing

"Where is the autopilot disconnect button located?"

Answer: On the control column

"What colour are the three lights when the undercarriage is down and locked?"

Answer: Green

"What call does Captain Jack make to get the flaps fully deployed?"

Answer: Full Flaps

"What does Captain Jack have to decide at the Decision Height?"

Answer: Whether he can see the runway and whether he is happy to continue the descent

"If he cannot land, what procedure does Captain Jack follow?"

Answer: Go-Around procedure

"At what height does the radio altimeter begin giving heights?"

Answer: At 300 feet

"What term does the radio altimeter use to tell Captain Jack to pull the engines back to idle?"

Answer: Retard

"Which part of the undercarriage must touch the runway first?"

Answer: The main wheels followed by the nose-wheel

"What is the main way of slowing an airliner after landing called?"

Answer: Reverse Thrust

Arrival and Deplaning

"What call orders the passenger doors to be disarmed?"

Answer: Doors to Manual

"What does the engineer put against the aircraft wheels to stop them moving when parked at the stand?"

Answer: Chocks

"What is the final checklist called?"

Answer: Shut Down checklist

Captain Jack says…

"Good luck with your dream of becoming a pilot."

Flying your Dream

Further books and information
can be found at

www.johnpullenwriter.com

Printed in Great Britain
by Amazon